BASIC

TACTICS FOR LISTENING

Second Edition

Jack C. Richards

OXFORD
UNIVERSITY PRESS

OXFORD
UNIVERSITY PRESS

198 Madison Avenue
New York, NY 10016 USA

Great Clarendon Street
Oxford OX2 6DP England

Oxford New York

Auckland Cape Town Dar es Salaam Hong Kong Karachi
Kuala Lumpur Madrid Melbourne Mexico City Nairobi
New Delhi Shanghai Taipei Toronto

With offices in

Argentina Austria Brazil Chile Czech Republic France Greece
Guatemala Hungary Italy Japan South Korea Poland Portugal
Singapore Switzerland Thailand Turkey Ukraine Vietnam

OXFORD is a trademark of Oxford University Press.

ISBN-13: 978 0 19 438451 3 (Student Book with CD pack)
ISBN-10: 0 19 438451 9

ISBN-13: 978 0 19 438842 9 (Student Book without CD)
ISBN-10: 0 19 438842 5

Editorial Manager: Nancy Leonhardt
Managing Editor: Jeff Krum
Editor: Joseph McGasko
Associate Editor: Amy Hawley
Art Director: Lynn Luchetti
Design Project Manager: Maj-Britt Hagsted
Senior Art Editor: Jodi Waxman
Production Manager: Shanta Persaud
Production Coordinator: Eve Wong

Printing (last digit): 10 9 8 7 6 5 4

Printed in Hong Kong.

Acknowledgments

Cover design: Lee Anne Dollison, Maj-Britt Hagsted
Cover photography: Arnold Katz Photography; PhotoDisc;
MPTA Stock/Masterfile; Barbara Haynor/Index Stock

Illustrations and Realia: Barbara Bastian, Kenneth Batelman,
Ron Bell, Wendy Caporale, Carlos Castellanos, Mike Deitz,
Jim DeLapine, Julie Ecklund, Robert Kuester, Susan Melrath,
Vilma Ortiz-Dillon, Leif Peng/IllustrationOnline.com,
Steve Sanford, Jeff Seaver, Kirsten Soderlind, Nina Wallace

The publishers would like to thank the following for their
permission to reproduce photographs:

H. Abernathy/H. Armstrong Roberts, Age Fotostock, Alamy
Images, Alberni/Age Fotostock, Daniel Aubry/The Stock Market,
Paul Barton/Corbis, W. Bertsch/H. Armstrong Roberts, Comstock,
Corbis, Peter Correz/Tony Stone Images, Cotla/Liason International,
Thomas Croke/Liason International, John de Visser/Masterfile,
Leo deWys/Pictures Colour Library, Chad Ehlers/International Stock,
Ed Elberfeld/Uniphoto, Jon Feingersh/The Stock Market, Curt
Fischer/Tony Stone Images, Graham French/Masterfile,
Gebhardt/Mauritius/H. Armstrong Roberts, Mitchell Gerber/Corbis,
Getty Images, H. Armstrong Roberts, John Henley/The Stock
Market,Thomas Hoeffgen/Getty Images, The Image Bank,
ImageState, Index Stock Imagery, Bob Krist/Corbis, Ralph
Krubner/H. Armstrong Roberts, Regis Lefebure/The Stock Market,
Rob Lewine Photography/Corbis, Dan Lim/Masterfile,
Malignon/Liason International, J. Malone/Jon Arnold Images,
Maratea/International Stock, Masterfile, Fred McKinney/FPG, John
Michael/International Stock, Benn Mitchell/The Image Bank, Warren
Morgan/H. Armstrong Roberts, Roy Morsch/The Stock Market, Mug
Shots/The Stock Market, Roy Ooms/Masterfile, Robert Young
Pelton/Corbis, PhotoDisc, Photofest, Photofest/Jagarts,
Photolink/PhotoDisc/PictureQuest, Stacy Pickerell/Tony Stone
Images, Pictor Images, PictureQuest, David Pollack/The Stock
Market, Alec Pytolwany/Masterfile, Kip Rano/Liason International,
Reuters, Reuters New Media, Inc./Corbis, Steve Schapiro/Liason
International, SIE Productions/Corbis, Sotographs/The Stock Market,
Paul A. Souders/Corbis, Paul Steel/The Stock Market, Tom
Stewart/The Stock Market, Johnny Stockshooter/International Stock,
Stone, Ken Straiton/The Stock Market, Vince Streano/Corbis, Taxi,
Paul Thompson/International Stock, Uniphoto, Monica Wells/Pictures
Colour Library, Larry Williams/Masterfile, Brent Winebrenner/
International Stock, Bobbe Wolf/International Stock

Contents

Scope and Sequence

Unit	Themes	Skills
1	Names Spelling Titles	Listening for names Listening for details Listening for formal and informal forms of address
2	People Physical appearance	Listening for topics Listening for gist Listening for details
3	Clothes	Listening for gist Listening for details
4	Time Numbers	Listening for times Listening for numbers Listening for letters and numbers
5	Dates	Listening for dates Listening for dates and times Listening for details Listening for gist
6	Jobs	Listening for gist Listening for details Listening for attitudes
7	Sports Exercise	Listening for gist Listening and making predictions Listening for frequency Listening for details
8	Locations Household objects	Listening for gist Listening for details Listening and making predictions
9	Family	Listening for gist Listening for details Listening for similarities
10	Entertainment Invitations	Listening for gist Listening for details Listening for acceptances and refusals
11	Prices Money Shopping	Listening for details Listening for gist
12	Restaurants Food	Listening for details Listening for gist Listening for attitudes

Unit	Themes	Skills
13	Greetings Socializing Parties	Listening for greetings and conversation endings Listening for topics Listening for details Listening for reactions
14	Vacations	Listening for gist Listening for attitudes Listening for details
15	Apartments Rooms Furniture	Listening for gist Listening for details
16	Movies Invitations	Listening for likes and dislikes Listening for gist Listening for attitudes Listening for opinions Listening for details
17	Weather Climate	Listening for gist Listening for details Listening and making predictions
18	Shopping	Listening for gist Listening and making predictions Listening for details
19	Using the telephone	Listening for gist Listening for details Listening for attitudes
20	Objects Possessions	Listening for gist Listening for details
21	Directions Streets Places	Listening for gist Listening for details Listening for sequence
22	People Friends	Listening for gist Listening for similarities and differences Listening for details Listening for opinions Listening for attitudes
23	Countries Cities	Listening for attitudes Listening for gist Listening for details Listening for preferences
24	Health Illnesses	Listening for gist Listening for details Listening for advice

Introduction

Tactics for Listening

Tactics for Listening is a three-level series of listening textbooks for students of English as a second or foreign language. Taken together, the three levels make up a comprehensive course in listening skills in American English.

Basic Tactics for Listening

Basic Tactics for Listening is the first level of the *Tactics for Listening* series. It is intended for students who have studied English previously but need further practice in understanding simple conversational language. It contains 24 units. It can be used as the main text for a listening course, as a complementary text in a conversation course, or as the basis for a language laboratory course. Each unit features a topic that relates to the everyday life and experience of adults and young adults. The topics have been chosen for their frequency in conversation and their interest to learners. A wide variety of stimulating and useful activities are included to give students graded practice in listening.

Student Book

In the *Basic Tactics for Listening* Student Book, students practice listening for a variety of purposes and hear examples of different types of spoken English including casual conversations, instructions, directions, requests, descriptions, apologies, and suggestions. Essential listening skills are practiced throughout the text. These skills include listening for key words, details, and gist; listening and making inferences; listening for attitudes; listening to questions and responding; and recognizing and identifying information.

Each unit has five sections. The first section, "Getting Ready," introduces the topic of the unit and presents key vocabulary for the unit listening tasks. The next three sections, each entitled "Let's Listen," are linked to conversations or monologues recorded on cassette or CD. These sections provide task-based, graded listening practice. Finally, there is a follow-up speaking activity, "Over to You," which relates to the theme and listening tasks of the unit.

Audio Program

The complete audio program for *Basic Tactics for Listening* Student Book is available as a set of three Class CDs or Cassettes. In addition, the Student Book with CD contains a Student CD on the inside back cover for home study. The CD includes the listening passages for the final Let's Listen section of each unit.

Teacher's Book

The *Basic Tactics for Listening* Teacher's Book provides extensive lesson plans for each unit, answer keys, optional activities, vocabulary lists, and a photocopiable tapescript of the recorded material. The Teacher's Book also includes photocopiable midterm and final tests, as well as worksheets (one per unit) that offer additional speaking activities. The audio program for the midterm and final tests is included on a CD on the inside back cover.

Test Booklet

The *Basic Tactics for Listening* Test Booklet contains photocopiable tests for each unit of the Student Book. The audio program for the unit tests is included on a CD on the inside back cover.

UNIT 1 Names and Titles

1. Getting Ready

Are these first names or last names? Write them in the chart. Then add two more names to each list.

David	Kennedy	Susan	Cruise	Nancy	Bob
Brian	Abrams	Jackson	Smith	Wilson	Tom

First names		Last names	
David	_____	Kennedy	_____
_____	_____	_____	_____
_____	_____	_____	_____
_____	_____	_____	_____

2. Let's Listen

What is the correct name of the hotel guest? Circle the correct answer.

1. a. Mary Carter
   b. Maria Carter

2. a. Suzanna Smith
   b. Susan Smith

3. a. Harry Wilson
   b. Harvey Wilson

4. a. Joseph Abrams
   b. Joseph Abramson

5. a. Louis Jackson
   b. Louise Jackson

6. a. Marlene Cruise
   b. Marley Cruise

3. Let's Listen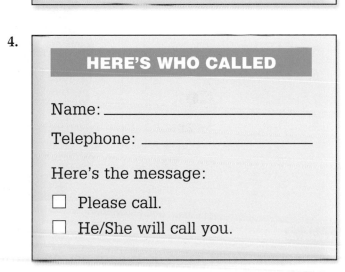

Task 1

Cindy's father is taking phone messages for her. Listen and complete the forms.

1.

HERE'S WHO CALLED

Name: _____

Telephone: _____

Here's the message:

☐ Please call.

☐ He/She will call you.

2.

HERE'S WHO CALLED

Name: _____

Telephone: _____

Here's the message:

☐ Please call.

☐ He/She will call you.

3.

HERE'S WHO CALLED

Name: _____

Telephone: _____

Here's the message:

☐ Please call.

☐ He/She will call you.

4.

HERE'S WHO CALLED

Name: _____

Telephone: _____

Here's the message:

☐ Please call.

☐ He/She will call you.

Task 2

Listen again. Circle the correct answer.

1. Bob knows Cindy from _____.

   a. work
   b. school
   c. home

2. _____ is the person who answers the phone.

   a. Tom
   b. Cindy
   c. Nancy

3. Cindy can't take the call because she is _____.

   a. busy
   b. asleep
   c. not home

4. The caller is Cindy's _____.

   a. boss
   b. teacher
   c. friend

4. Let's Listen 💿

We usually use a title (Ms., Mr., Mrs., Miss, Dr., Professor) with a last name, but not with a first name, in formal greetings.

	Correct	**Incorrect**
Formal:	Good morning, Ms. Smith.	✗ Good morning, Ms. Mary.
Informal:	Good morning, Mary.	✗ Good morning, Smith.

Listen. Are the woman's greetings formal or informal? Check (✓) the correct answer.

	Formal	Informal
1.	☐	✓
2.	☐	☐
3.	☐	☐
4.	☐	☐
5.	☐	☐
6.	☐	☐
7.	☐	☐
8.	☐	☐

Task 2

Listen again. What name does each person use? Circle the correct answer.

1. a. Damien
   b. David

2. a. Jackson
   b. Johnson

3. a. Rob
   b. Bob

4. a. Michelle
   b. Marcia

5. a. Smith
   b. Schmidt

6. a. James
   b. John

7. a. Abrams
   b. Abraham

8. a. Steinway
   b. Steinberg

Over to You: What's your name?

Talk to four classmates. Find out their names and telephone numbers.
Ask these questions and write the answers in the chart.

Excuse me. What's your first name?

How do you spell that?

What's your last name?

What's your telephone number?

	First name	Last name	Telephone number
1.			
2.			
3.			
4.			

Task 2

Choose the name of a famous person. Talk to three classmates and find out the names they chose.

Example: A: Who did you choose?

B: I chose _____.

A: How do you spell that?

B: _____.

UNIT 2 Describing People

1. Getting Ready

Are these words and phrases about age, height, or hair? Write them in the correct lists.

short	about 22	about 170 cm	in her teens	dark	almost 25
long	19 years old	blond	tall	curly	straight
in his twenties	light brown	in her thirties	not so tall	shoulder-length	

Age	Height	Hair
_____	_____	*short*
_____	_____	_____
_____	_____	_____
_____	_____	_____
_____	_____	_____
_____	_____	_____
_____	_____	_____
_____	_____	_____

2. Let's Listen

People are describing other people. What are they describing? Listen and check (✓) the correct answer.

	Age	Height	Hair
1.	✓	☐	☐
2.	☐	☐	☐
3.	☐	☐	☐
4.	☐	☐	☐
5.	☐	☐	☐
6.	☐	☐	☐
7.	☐	☐	☐
8.	☐	☐	☐

3. Let's Listen

Listen to these descriptions of people. Check (✓) the correct picture.

1.

a.   b.

2.
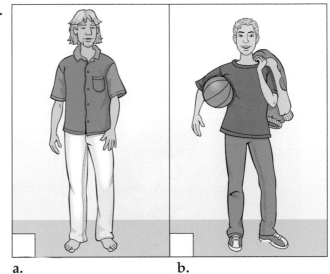
a.   b.

3.

a.   b.

4.

a.   b.

Task 2

Listen again. Are these statements true or false? Check (✓) the correct answer.

		True	False
1.	Cindy isn't so tall.	☐	☐
2.	Bob is in his teens.	☐	☐
3.	Anne is 29.	☐	☐
4.	Paul's cousin has blond hair.	☐	☐

4. Let's Listen 💿

Task 1

Some parents are looking for their children in a department store. Listen and
write each child's age.

1. _7_   2. _____   3. _____   4. _____   5. _____

Task 2

Listen again. Which child is being described? Number the pictures.

A.

B.

C.

D.

E.

Over to You: Who is it?

Task 1

Work in pairs. Take turns describing people in the pictures and guessing who they are.

Example: **A:** This man is about 30.

B: Does he have dark hair?

A: No, he doesn't.

B: Is he tall?

A: Yes, he is.

B: Is it Jay?

A: Yes, it is.

Jay / Sarah

John / Doris

Tom / Billy

Maria / Stan

Task 2

Take turns describing two people in your class and guessing who they are.

Example: **A:** She has short hair.

B: Is it Keiko?

A: No, it isn't. She's tall.

B: Is it…?

UNIT 3 Clothes

1. Getting Ready

Match each word with a picture. Write the correct letter.

1. jeans _A_   5. dress ___   9. hat ___   13. glasses ___   17. blouse ___

2. tie ___   6. scarf ___   10. suit ___   14. pants ___   18. shoulder bag ___

3. sandals ___   7. windbreaker ___ 11. shorts ___   15. shirt ___

4. jacket ___   8. skirt ___   12. T-shirt ___   16. sneakers ___

2. Let's Listen

Sandra is describing the people at her party. Which person is she describing?
Listen and write the correct letter.

1. David _F_

2. Janet ___

3. Ron ___

4. Barbara ___

5. Andy ___

6. Patty ___

7. Mary ___

8. Ken ___

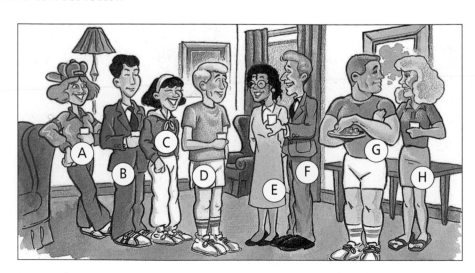

3. Let's Listen

Task 1

People are trying on clothes in a department store. Listen and number the pictures.

A. ☐

B. ☐ /

C. ☐

D. ☐

E. ☐

F. ☐

Task 2

Listen again. What does each person need? Circle the correct answer.

1. He needs to find a _____ pair.

   a. longer
   b. shorter
   c. cheaper

2. She needs to find a _____ one.

   a. prettier
   b. bigger
   c. smaller

3. She needs to find a _____ pair.

   a. tighter
   b. bigger
   c. smaller

4. He needs to find a _____ pair.

   a. bigger
   b. cheaper
   c. smaller

5. He needs to find a _____ one.

   a. tighter
   b. looser
   c. smaller

6. She needs to find a _____ size.

   a. smaller
   b. bigger
   c. more comfortable

4. Let's Listen

Does the information you hear match the description? Listen and check (✓) the correct answer.

	Correct	Incorrect
1. Sonia		
a. no jacket	☐	☑
b. bag	☐	☐
c. no earrings	☐	☐
d. black shoes	☐	☐
2. Brian		
a. new jeans	☐	☐
b. T-shirt	☐	☐
c. scarf	☐	☐
d. no rings	☐	☐
3. Kevin		
a. shirt	☐	☐
b. no tie	☐	☐
c. pants	☐	☐
d. shoulder bag	☐	☐
4. Mrs. Graham		
a. skirt	☐	☐
b. no jewelry	☐	☐
c. bag	☐	☐
d. sandals	☐	☐

Task 2

Listen again. What was each person wearing? Circle the correct answer.

1. Sonia was wearing a _____ skirt.

   a. yellow
   b. black
   c. dark blue

2. Brian was wearing a _____ belt.

   a. red
   b. wide
   c. silver

3. Kevin was wearing _____ pants.

   a. brown
   b. white
   c. green

4. Mrs. Graham was wearing a _____ scarf.

   a. long
   b. black
   c. beautiful

Over to You: What is she wearing?

Task 1

Work in pairs. Take turns describing people at a party and guessing who they are. Say what each person is wearing.

Example: A: This woman is wearing a skirt.

B: Is she wearing a T-shirt?

A: No, she isn't.

B: Is she wearing glasses?

A: No, she isn't.

B: Is she wearing a scarf?

A: Yes, she is.

B: Is it Monica?

A: Yes, it is.

Monica   Kim   David   Barbara   Larry   Joyce

Task 2

Work in pairs. Look at your partner for 30 seconds. Then sit back-to-back. Try to describe what your partner is wearing. How many things can you remember?

UNIT 4 Time

1. Getting Ready

Task 1

Match each time with a picture. Write the number.

1. twenty to two
2. three fifteen
3. ten after ten
4. two twenty
5. three fifty-five
6. six forty-five
7. two o'clock
8. five past ten

A.    B. 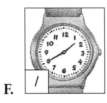   C. 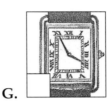   D.

E.   F. /   G.   H.

Task 2

Can you say these times?

1.    2.    3.

2. Let's Listen

Listen and write the correct time on each clock.

1.  10 : 15   2.  :   3.  :

4. :    5.  :   6. :

3. Let's Listen

Task 1

Listen to these radio announcements. Circle the correct time.

1. a. 7:50
   b. 7:15

2. a. 10:45
   b. 10:05

3. a. 1:59
   b. 2:05

4. a. 11:10
   b. 11:02

5. a. 6:55
   b. 6:15

6. a. 1:40
   b. 1:14

7. a. 9:30
   b. 9:13

8. a. 5:55
   b. 5:05

Task 2

Listen again and circle the correct radio station.

1. a. 19.9
   b. 90.9
   c. 99.9

2. a. 10.05
   b. 109.1
   c. 105.1

3. a. 698.9
   b. X98.5
   c. H98.5

4. a. WXYZ
   b. WWYZ
   c. UXYZ

5. a. NBC
   b. BBC
   c. BBD

6. a. WQXR
   b. W2XR
   c. W26R

7. a. 1010
   b. 1001
   c. 99.30

8. a. KCBB
   b. KABC
   c. QABC

4. Let's Listen

Task 1

People are calling about show times for movies. Listen and write the show times you hear.

1.

Times
3:40
_____
_____
_____

2.

Times
_____
_____
_____
_____

3.

Times
_____
_____
_____
_____

4.

Times
_____
_____
_____
_____

Task 2

Listen again. Write the times.

1. The box office opens at _____.

2. The coffee bar is open from _____ to _____.

3. The sneak preview begins at _____.

4. The box office closes at _____.

Over to You: What time is it in...?

Look at the time in each city.

New York / 8 a.m. / Friday

Paris / 2 p.m. / Friday

Tokyo / 10 p.m. / Friday

What is the time difference between the cities? Write the correct number.

1. New York and Paris? _____ hours

2. Paris and Tokyo? _____ hours

3. New York and Tokyo? _____ hours

Task 2

Work in pairs. Take turns asking about times in New York, Paris, and Tokyo. Write the answers in the charts.

Example: **A:** It's 8 a.m. on Friday in New York. What time is it in Paris?

B: It's 2 p.m. on Friday.

A: So what time is it in Tokyo?

B: It's 10 p.m. on Friday.

New York	Paris	Tokyo
8 a.m. Friday	2 p.m. Friday	10 p.m. Friday
	2 p.m. Saturday	
		7 p.m. Sunday
5 p.m. Monday		
12 p.m. Tuesday		

UNIT 5 Dates

1. Getting Ready

JANUARY	FEBRUARY	MARCH	APRIL	MAY	JUNE
S M T W T F S	S M T W T F S	S M T W T F S	S M T W T F S	S M T W T F S	S M T W T F S

JANUARY
S M T W T F S
1 2 3
4 5 6 7 8 9 10
11 12 13 14 15 16 17
18 19 20 21 22 23 24
25 26 27 28 29 30 31

FEBRUARY
S M T W T F S
1 2 3 4 5 6 7
8 9 10 11 12 13 14
15 16 17 18 19 20 21
22 23 24 25 26 27 28

MARCH
S M T W T F S
1 2 3 4 5 6 7
8 9 10 11 12 13 14
15 16 17 18 19 20 21
22 23 24 25 26 27 28
29 30 31

APRIL
S M T W T F S
1 2 3 4
5 6 7 8 9 10 11
12 13 14 15 16 17 18
19 20 21 22 23 24 25
26 27 28 29 30

MAY
S M T W T F S
1 2
3 4 5 6 7 8 9
10 11 12 13 14 15 16
17 18 19 20 21 22 23
24 25 26 27 28 29 30
31

JUNE
S M T W T F S
1 2 3 4 5 6
7 8 9 10 11 12 13
14 15 16 17 18 19 20
21 22 23 24 25 26 27
28 29 30

JULY
S M T W T F S
1 2 3 4
5 6 7 8 9 10 11
12 13 14 15 16 17 18
19 20 21 22 23 24 25
26 27 28 29 30 31

AUGUST
S M T W T F S
1
2 3 4 5 6 7 8
9 10 11 12 13 14 15
16 17 18 19 20 21 22
23 24 25 26 27 28 29
30 31

SEPTEMBER
S M T W T F S
1 2 3 4 5
6 7 8 9 10 11 12
13 14 15 16 17 18 19
20 21 22 23 24 25 26
27 28 29 30

OCTOBER
S M T W T F S
1 2 3
4 5 6 7 8 9 10
11 12 13 14 15 16 17
18 19 20 21 22 23 24
25 26 27 28 29 30 31

NOVEMBER
S M T W T F S
1 2 3 4 5 6 7
8 9 10 11 12 13 14
15 16 17 18 19 20 21
22 23 24 25 26 27 28
29 30

DECEMBER
S M T W T F S
1 2 3 4 5
6 7 8 9 10 11 12
13 14 15 16 17 18 19
20 21 22 23 24 25 26
27 28 29 30 31

Task 1

Match the dates on the left with the dates on the right.

1. 3/2/01 _c_
2. 6/11/99 ___
3. 11/1/92 ___
4. 5/20/95 ___
5. 2/28/03 ___

a. November first, nineteen ninety-two
b. May twentieth, nineteen ninety-five
c. March second, two thousand one
d. February twenty-eighth, two thousand three
e. June eleventh, nineteen ninety-nine

Task 2

Write your birthday and a classmate's birthday.

_____ _____

2. Let's Listen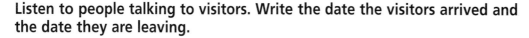

Listen to people talking to visitors. Write the date the visitors arrived and the date they are leaving.

	Arrived	Will Leave
1.	1	14
2.		
3.		
4.		
5.		
6.		

JULY						
S	M	T	W	T	F	S
			1	2	3	4
5	6	7	8	9	10	11
12	13	14	15	16	17	18
19	20	21	22	23	24	25
26	27	28	29	30	31	

3. Let's Listen

Don is checking messages on his voicemail. Listen and write the date and time of each event.

	Date	Time
1. dental appointment	8/3	9:30 a.m.
2. Cindy's party		
3. aunt's arrival		
4. tennis game		
5. meeting with Francis		
6. trip		

Listen again. Are these statements true or false? Check (✓) the correct answer.

	True	False
1. The caller is confirming Don's appointment.	☐	☐
2. Sue will call Don later.	☐	☐
3. Don's aunt will call him from the hotel.	☐	☐
4. Ted and Don are going to play tennis on Saturday.	☐	☐
5. Francis wants to meet Don in the office.	☐	☐
6. The flight leaves from the airport in New Orleans.	☐	☐

4. Let's Listen 💿

Task 1

Listen to people talking about their birthdays. Have they had their birthdays yet this year?
Check (✓) the correct answer.

	Yes	No
1. Ted	☐	☐
2. Jill	☐	☐
3. Sue	☐	☐
4. Brian	☐	☐

Task 2

Listen again. What activity did each person do or will each person do for his or her birthday?
Circle the correct answer.

1. **Ted**

   a. have a party
   b. study for exams
   c. meet friends

2. **Jill**

   a. go to her parents' house
   b. go on a trip by herself
   c. go to New York with her parents

3. **Sue**

   a. have a barbecue
   b. go out to dinner with friends
   c. stay home alone

4. **Brian**

   a. meet friends
   b. have a busy day
   c. have a quiet family party

Over to You: When's your birthday?

Task 1

Move around the class and find out your classmates' birthdays. Circle each person's birthday on the calendar.

Example: **A:** When's your birthday?

             B: It's on August 16th. When's yours?

             A: It's on _____ .

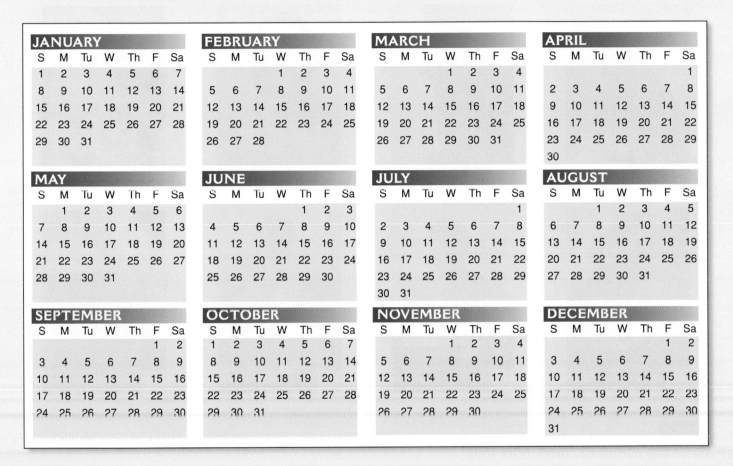

Task 2

Work in pairs. Answer the questions.

How many people...?	Number
have their birthdays in the same month	_____
have a birthday this month	_____
have a birthday next month	_____
have the same birthday	_____
have the same birthday as you	_____

UNIT 6 Jobs

1. Getting Ready

Task 1

Match each job with a picture. Write the number.

1. businessperson
2. nurse
3. taxi driver
4. chef
5. waitress
6. flight attendant
7. construction worker
8. teacher

 A.

 B.

 C.

 D.

 E.

 F. /

 G.

 H.

Task 2

Write the names of three more jobs.

_____   _____   _____

2. Let's Listen

People are talking about work. What job are they talking about? Listen and circle the correct answer.

1. a. salesperson
   b. office worker

2. a. waiter
   b. actor

3. a. teacher
   b. flight attendant

4. a. chef
   b. nurse

5. a. nurse
   b. businessperson

6. a. receptionist
   b. construction worker

3. Let's Listen

Task 1

Listen to people talking about their work. Check (✓) the correct information about each person.

	Has the same job	Has a new job	Isn't working now
1. Ted	☐	☐	☐
2. Sonia	☐	☐	☐
3. Bob	☐	☐	☐
4. Marie	☐	☐	☐
5. Suzanne	☐	☐	☐
6. Martha	☐	☐	☐
7. Fred	☐	☐	☐
8. Sue	☐	☐	☐

Task 2

Listen again. Match the people on the left with the information on the right.

1. Ted ___   **a.** is a teacher.

2. Sonia ___   **b.** just graduated from college.

3. Bob ___   **c.** is trying to find a new job.

4. Marie ___   **d.** works in a bookstore.

5. Suzanne ___   **e.** works in a bank.

6. Martha ___   **f.** works in a restaurant.

7. Fred ___   **g.** is a receptionist.

8. Sue ___   **h.** is a lawyer.

4. Let's Listen

Task 1

Listen to people talking about their jobs. Do they like their jobs?
Check (✓) the correct answer.

	Yes	No
1.	☐	☑
2.	☐	☐
3.	☐	☐
4.	☐	☐
5.	☐	☐

Task 2

Listen again. What do the people like or dislike about their jobs?
Check (✓) the correct answer.

			Likes	Dislikes
1.	a.	doing the same thing	☐	☐
	b.	the money	☐	☐
2.	a.	working with kids	☐	☐
	b.	the distance to school	☐	☐
3.	a.	the people	☐	☐
	b.	the travel	☐	☐
4.	a.	the hours	☐	☐
	b.	her boss	☐	☐
5.	a.	being on his feet	☐	☐
	b.	the tips	☐	☐

Over to You: What do you do?

Work in groups of four. Choose one of the jobs below or use one of your own ideas. The other people in the group ask you Yes/No questions and try to guess the job.

Examples: Do you work inside?

Is it a dangerous job?

Do you wear a uniform?

Are you a _____?

deep-sea diver

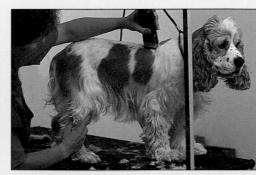
dog groomer

rock musician

soldier

puppeteer

window washer

Your idea: _____

UNIT 7 Sports and Exercise

1. Getting Ready

Do you ever do any of these things? Check (✓) your answers and compare them with a partner.

You	Yes	No
windsurf	☐	☐
play baseball	☐	☐
ski	☐	☐
play golf	☐	☐
go to a gym	☐	☐
play tennis	☐	☐
walk	☐	☐
play volleyball	☐	☐
swim	☐	☐
play football	☐	☐
ride a bike	☐	☐
other: _____	☐	☐

Your partner	Yes	No
windsurf	☐	☐
play baseball	☐	☐
ski	☐	☐
play golf	☐	☐
go to a gym	☐	☐
play tennis	☐	☐
walk	☐	☐
play volleyball	☐	☐
swim	☐	☐
play football	☐	☐
ride a bike	☐	☐
other: _____	☐	☐

2. Let's Listen

People are talking about sports and exercise. Listen and number the pictures.

A. ☐

B. ☐

C. ☐

D. ☐

E. ☐

F. ☐

3. Let's Listen

Which sports or activities is the person talking about? Listen and circle the correct answer.

1. a. swimming
   b. going to the gym
   c. jogging

2. a. playing volleyball
   b. playing golf
   c. playing soccer

3. a. playing baseball
   b. playing football
   c. playing tennis

4. a. playing tennis
   b. watching TV
   c. reading

5. a. swimming
   b. jogging
   c. windsurfing

6. a. diving
   b. riding a bicycle
   c. walking

Task 2

Listen again. What do you think each person says next? Circle the correct answer.

1. a. Yes, about three times a week.
   b. Yeah, I'm getting lazy.
   c. Yeah, I'm tired.

2. a. Yeah, I'm very busy.
   b. Yeah, I'd love to.
   c. Yeah, you're right.

3. a. Volleyball is tiring.
   b. Volleyball. It's my favorite.
   c. Tennis is expensive.

4. a. I know, but I'm lazy.
   b. No, thanks. I'm tired.
   c. Yeah, reading is fun.

5. a. It's too hot.
   b. I enjoy skiing.
   c. I don't like the cold.

6. a. In the car.
   b. In the morning.
   c. In the park.

4. Let's Listen

Task 1

Listen to people talking about how they spend their free time. Check (✓) the correct information about each person.

	Exercises a lot	Exercises a little	Never exercises
1. Bill	✔	☐	☐
2. Liz	☐	☐	☐
3. Victor	☐	☐	☐
4. Maria	☐	☐	☐
5. David	☐	☐	☐

Task 2

Listen again. Match the people on the left with the activities on the right.

1. Bill ___   a. golfs

2. Liz ___   b. bicycles

3. Victor ___   c. plays baseball

4. Maria ___   d. takes walks

5. David ___   e. plays video games

Over to You: What do you want to do?

Task 1

Read the questions in the chart and check (✓) your answers. Then ask a classmate the questions and circle the activities that both of you want to do.

Do you want to...?	Yes	No
do karate	☐	☐
play golf	☐	☐
water-ski	☐	☐
windsurf	☐	☐
ski	☐	☐
play tennis	☐	☐
play soccer	☐	☐
go rock climbing	☐	☐
ride a horse	☐	☐
do judo	☐	☐
swim	☐	☐

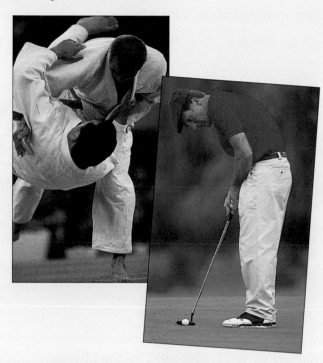

Task 2

Move around the class and find someone who can do each activity. Write his or her name in the chart.

Can you...?	Name
do karate	_____
play golf	_____
water-ski	_____
windsurf	_____
ski	_____
play tennis	_____
play soccer	_____
go rock climbing	_____
ride a horse	_____
do judo	_____
swim	_____

UNIT 8 Locations

1. Getting Ready

Task 1

Find each item in the picture. Write the number in the correct box.

1. a plant **2.** the skis **3.** the bed **4.** the golf clubs **5.** a book **6.** the newspaper

Task 2

Write the number of each item next to the phrase.

___ behind the TV   ___ on the table   ___ between the bedside tables

___ on top of the bookshelf   ___ next to the window   ___ under the table

2. Let's Listen

Some people are asking where items are. Listen and check (✓) the correct picture.

1.

    a.   b.

2.
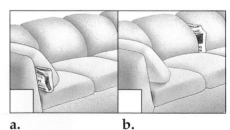

    a.   b.

3.

    a.   b.

4.
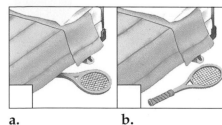

    a.   b.

3. Let's Listen

Task 1

Pat is helping Tom decorate his new apartment. Listen and write the number in the location she suggests.

1. the magazine rack
2. the coffee table
3. the plant stand
4. the bookshelf
5. the chair
6. the end table
7. the TV
8. the dinner table

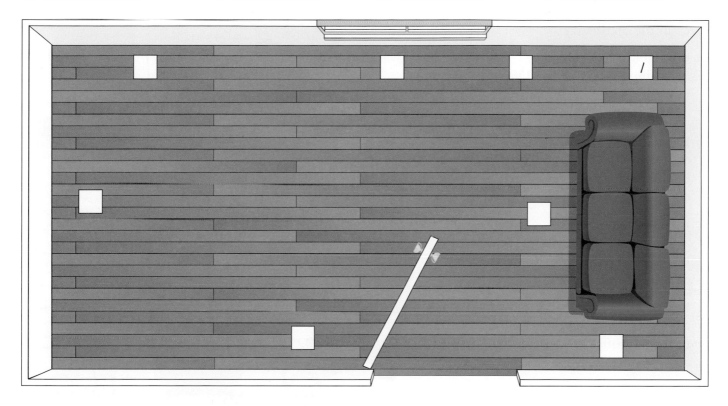

Task 2

Listen again. What do you think each person says next? Circle the correct answer.

1. **a.** Yes, it is.
   b. Yes, I agree, it will.
   c. Yes, it does.

2. **a.** Yes, they are.
   b. Yes, it can.
   c. Yes, I think so, too.

3. **a.** Okay. Try that.
   b. Of course not.
   c. No, I don't.

4. **a.** Yes, it will.
   b. No, the other one.
   c. Yes, it will look good there.

5. **a.** Yes, I will.
   b. Yeah. That's right.
   c. Yes, it does.

6. **a.** Yes, it can.
   b. Yes, that's perfect.
   c. Yes, it does.

7. **a.** Yes, it will.
   b. Yes, it does.
   c. It looks fine.

8. **a.** Yes. That's right.
   b. Of course it can.
   c. No, it doesn't.

4. Let's Listen

Task 1

Tony is helping Cindy clean up the house. Where should he put the items?
Listen and circle the correct answer.

1. **the magazines**
   a. on the bookshelf on top of the dictionary
   b. on the bookshelf next to the dictionary
   c. in the dictionary

2. **the remote control**
   a. beside the TV on the TV program guide
   b. on top of the TV next to the TV program guide
   c. beside the TV program guide in front of the TV

3. **the keys**
   a. in a box on top of the desk
   b. in a box inside one of the desk drawers
   c. inside a drawer next to a box

4. **the baseball cap**
   a. on the hook behind the door
   b. on the doorknob
   c. on the floor behind the door

5. **the glasses**
   a. inside the case on the coffee table
   b. on the coffee table next to the papers
   c. on top of the papers on the coffee table

6. **the belt**
   a. on the sofa in front of the window
   b. on the chair next to the window
   c. on the floor next to the window

Task 2

Listen again. Are these statements true or false? Check (✓) the correct answer.

	True	False
1. Tony hasn't read the magazines.	☐	☐
2. The remote control has a new battery.	☐	☐
3. The keys are for the office.	☐	☐
4. The baseball cap belongs to Cindy's brother.	☐	☐
5. Cindy needs glasses for reading.	☐	☐
6. Cindy's brother is always very neat.	☐	☐

Over to You: Where are the shoes?

Task 1

One of you is Student A. The other is Student B.

Student A: Look at your list of items. Draw each item in a different place on Picture A.
Student B: Look at your list of items. Draw each item in a different place on Picture B.

Student A's list
a hat
glasses
a wallet

Picture A

Student B's list
a pair of shoes
a book
a candle

Picture B

Task 2

**Work in pairs. Where did your partner draw the items on his or her picture?
Ask questions and draw them on the other picture.**

Example: **A:** Where are the shoes?

B: The shoes are....

Where is the hat?

A: The hat is....

Task 3

Work in pairs. Compare your pictures. Are they the same?

UNIT 9 The Family

1. Getting Ready

Write the correct word next to each family member.

uncle	great-grandfather	cousin	aunt	grandparents	niece	nephew	mother-in-law

1. My mother's sister is my _aunt_ .

2. My father's brother is my _____.

3. My parents' parents are my _____.

4. My uncle's son or daughter is my _____.

5. My brother or sister's son is my _____.

6. My brother or sister's daughter is my _____.

7. My husband or wife's mother is my _____.

8. My grandmother or grandfather's father is my _____.

2. Let's Listen

People are talking about their families. Listen and number the pictures.

A.   B.   C.

D.   E.   F.

3. Let's Listen

People are talking about their families. How many brothers and sisters do they have?
Listen and write the numbers.

	Older brothers	Younger brothers	Older sisters	Younger sisters
1. Stephanie	0	0	3	0
2. Donna	—	—	—	—
3. Bob	—	—	—	—
4. Rosie	—	—	—	—
5. Tina	—	—	—	—

Task 2

Listen again. Circle the correct answer.

1. Stephanie would like to have _____.

   a. brothers
   b. sisters
   c. cousins

2. Donna's brother is a _____.

   a. teacher
   b. student
   c. professor

3. Bob's sister _____ bosses him around.

   a. never
   b. sometimes
   c. always

4. Rosie's friend would like to come from a _____ family.

   a. small
   b. big
   c. medium-size

5. Tina is _____ child.

   a. an only
   b. a lonely
   c. one

4. Let's Listen 💿

Task 1

People are talking about themselves and other family members. Which family member is the speaker most similar to? Listen and check (✓) the correct answer.

	Father	Mother	Sister	Brother
1. Wen-ping	☐	☐	✓	☐
2. Michael	☐	☐	☐	☐
3. Justin	☐	☐	☐	☐
4. Susan	☐	☐	☐	☐
5. Robert	☐	☐	☐	☐
6. Beth	☐	☐	☐	☐

Task 2

Listen again. How is each family member different from the speaker? Write the letter.

1. Wen-ping's brother ___   a. likes sports.

2. Michael's brother ___   b. likes reading and music.

3. Justin's sister ___   c. is taller than the father.

4. Susan's father ___   d. prefers to play cards.

5. Robert's sister ___   e. hates flying.

6. Beth's father ___   f. isn't interested in music.

Over to You: Do you have any brothers or sisters?

Task 1

Look at this family tree. Then draw your own family tree on a piece of paper.
Explain your family tree to a classmate.

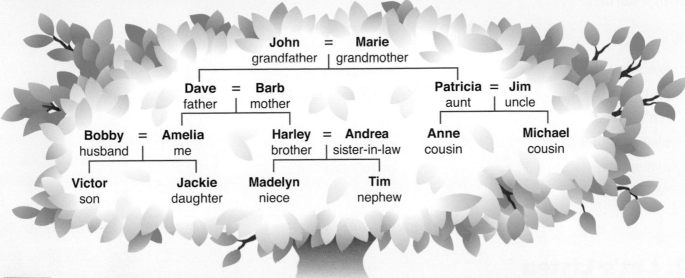

Task 2

Talk to two classmates and find out about their families. Write the information
in the chart.

Examples: Do you have any brothers?   Do you have a sister?

What are their names?   What is her name?

How old are they?   How old is she?

Classmate's name:		
Number of brothers	_____	_____
Names	_____	_____
Ages	_____	_____
Number of sisters	_____	_____
Names	_____	_____
Ages	_____	_____
Number of cousins	_____	_____
Names	_____	_____
Ages	_____	_____
Number of aunts and uncles	_____	_____
Names	_____	_____
Ages	_____	_____

UNIT 10 Entertainment

1. Getting Ready

What do you like to do on the weekend? Check (✓) your answers and compare them with a partner.

	Yes	No		Yes	No
exercise at the gym	☐	☐	go shopping	☐	☐
go to a movie	☐	☐	watch sports on TV	☐	☐
rent a video	☐	☐	go to a disco	☐	☐
play computer games	☐	☐	go to a park	☐	☐
play sports	☐	☐	go rollerblading	☐	☐
eat out	☐	☐	other: _____	☐	☐

2. Let's Listen

People are talking about entertainment. Listen and number the pictures.

A. ☐

B. ☐

C. ☐

D. ☐

E. ☐

F. ☐

3. Let's Listen

These people are calling friends about the weekend. Are these statements true or false?
Listen and check (✓) the correct answer.

	True	False
1. Penny agrees to go to a movie with Bob.	☐	☐
2. Anne can't come to the party.	☐	☐
3. Ken invites Nancy to a movie.	☐	☐
4. Anne and Mike are going to see a football game.	☐	☐
5. Wendy can't go to Jack's house.	☐	☐

Task 2

Listen again. Circle the correct answer for each question.

1. When does Bob want to go to the movies?

   a. on the weekend
   b. on Friday morning
   c. on Friday night

2. When is the party?

   a. on Saturday night
   b. the weekend after next
   c. on Sunday night

3. When does Ken want to go out with Nancy?

   a. on Friday morning
   b. on Friday night
   c. on the weekend

4. When is the game?

   a. on Sunday night
   b. on Sunday afternoon
   c. on Saturday afternoon

5. When is the movie on TV?

   a. Tuesday night
   b. Thursday night
   c. tonight

4. Let's Listen

Task 1

Listen to these invitations. Does the person accept or refuse? Check (✓) the correct answer.

		Accept	Refuse
1.	Bobby	☐	☑
2.	Melissa	☐	☐
3.	Jack	☐	☐
4.	Betty	☐	☐
5.	Ralph	☐	☐
6.	Jill	☐	☐

Task 2

Listen again. What is each invitation for? Circle the correct answer.

1. a. breakfast
    b. dinner
    c. coffee

2. a. a concert
    b. a play
    c. a movie

3. a. coffee
    b. lunch
    c. dinner

4. a. a party
    b. dinner
    c. a barbecue

5. a. tennis
    b. a drive
    c. a trip

6. a. a walk
    b. a party
    c. shopping

Over to You: Are you doing anything on Saturday?

Task 1

Work in pairs. Number the sentences to make two conversations. Then take turns practicing the conversations.

Conversation 1

A

___ Great. See you on Saturday, then.

___ *Police Academy 10.*

___ At 7:30 and 9:30.

_1_ Would you like to see a movie this Saturday?

___ Okay. What time do you want to meet?

B

___ Let's go to the 7:30 show.

_2_ Sure. What movie do you want to see?

___ Let's meet at 7:00 in front of the theater.

___ Great. What time does it start?

___ Yeah. See you on Saturday.

Conversation 2

A

___ Are you doing anything on Saturday?

___ Okay. See you at eight.

___ Yeah. Why don't we have a pizza or something?

___ Well, there's a rock concert. Do you feel like going?

___ It starts at around 9 o'clock.

B

___ Good idea. How about meeting at the pizza parlor at 8 o'clock?

___ See you then.

___ Sure. That sounds great. What time is the concert?

___ Okay. Maybe we could get something to eat before it starts.

___ No, not really.

Task 2

Work in pairs. Invite your partner to do one of the activities below with you. Arrange a time and a place to meet.

go to a movie   go to a disco   go shopping   go to a game   go for a drive

UNIT 11 Prices

1. Getting Ready

Can you guess the price of these items in a typical American city? Write the prices in the chart. Then write the prices of these items in your city.

75¢	$9	$18	$75	$250	$1,200

	American city's price	Your city's price
1. a movie ticket	$9	
2. a newspaper		
3. a digital camera		
4. a CD		
5. a pair of sneakers		
6. a laptop computer		

2. Let's Listen

Task 1

Listen to these people asking about prices. Write the price of each item.

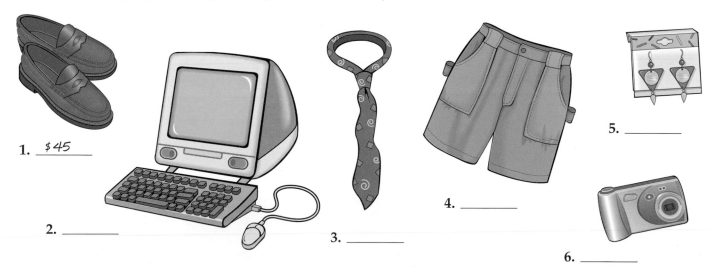

1. $45

2. _____

3. _____

4. _____

5. _____

6. _____

Task 2

Listen again. Did the person buy the item? Check (✓) the correct answer.

1. ☐ yes   2. ☐ yes   3. ☐ yes   4. ☐ yes   5. ☐ yes   6. ☐ yes
   ☐ no   ☐ no   ☐ no   ☐ no   ☐ no   ☐ no

3. Let's Listen

Listen to cashiers in a store. Write the total amount each person needs to pay and the amount of change each person receives.

1. total: _____ $7.50 _____

   change: _____ $12.50 _____

2. total: _____

   change: _____

3. total: _____

   change: _____

4. total: _____

   change: _____

5. total: _____

   change: _____

6. total: _____

   change: _____

Task 2

Listen again. Check (✓) the two things each person bought.

1. ☐ soup
   ☐ soap
   ☐ apples
   ☐ tomatoes
   ☐ shampoo

2. ☐ CD
   ☐ game
   ☐ video
   ☐ cassette
   ☐ poster

3. ☐ newspapers
   ☐ stamps
   ☐ books
   ☐ notebook
   ☐ magazines

4. ☐ coat
   ☐ T-shirt
   ☐ shoes
   ☐ socks
   ☐ tie

5. ☐ chocolates
   ☐ cake
   ☐ soda
   ☐ bread
   ☐ cookies

6. ☐ stamps
   ☐ magazines
   ☐ newspaper
   ☐ book
   ☐ notebook

4. Let's Listen

Task 1

Listen to people talking about prices in the U.S. and prices in their own country.
Check (✓) the correct answer.

	Cheaper in their country	Cheaper in the U.S.
1. cars	☐	☑
2. rents	☐	☐
3. clothes	☐	☐
4. air travel	☐	☐
5. tuition	☐	☐
6. hospitals	☐	☐

Task 2

Listen again. Are these statements true or false? Check (✓) the correct answer.

		True	False
1.	She doesn't own a car in the U.S.	☐	☐
2.	He lived in a nicer neighborhood at home than the one he lives in now.	☐	☐
3.	She bought a lot of clothes before she moved to the U.S.	☐	☐
4.	She travels by plane a lot in the U.S.	☐	☐
5.	Public schools in his country are better than those in the U.S.	☐	☐
6.	Hospitals and clinics are expensive in his country.	☐	☐

Over to You: How much do you spend?

How much do you spend each week on the following things? Complete the chart.

Item	Amount you spend each week
transportation	_____
clothes	_____
music	_____
snack food	_____
drinks	_____
magazines	_____
entertainment	_____
other: _____	_____

Task 2

Work in groups of three. Take turns asking the members of your group how much they spend. Write their answers in the chart. Then compare your answers with your classmates' answers.

Example: **A:** Keiko, how much do you usually spend a week on transportation?

B: About _____. How about you, Cindy?

C: About _____.

Item	Amount each week	
	Name _____	Name _____
transportation	_____	_____
clothes	_____	_____
music	_____	_____
snack food	_____	_____
drinks	_____	_____
magazines	_____	_____
entertainment	_____	_____
other: _____	_____	_____

UNIT 12 Restaurants

1. Getting Ready

Write the words below in the chart. Then add one more item to each list.

salad	apple pie	coffee	carrots	steak	peas	fish juice
cake	tea	chicken	ice cream	broccoli	soup	shrimp cocktail

Appetizers	Main dishes	Vegetables	Desserts	Drinks
salad	_____	_____	_____	_____
_____	_____	_____	_____	_____
_____	_____	_____	_____	_____
_____	_____	_____	_____	_____

2. Let's Listen

People are ordering food in a restaurant. Listen and check (✓) each person's order.

1.

MENU

Appetizers
☐ Vegetable soup   4.50
☐ House salad   3.75

Main Dishes
☐ Steak with fries   18.00
☐ Roast chicken   9.95
☐ Spaghetti with
   meat sauce   11.00

Desserts
☐ Apple pie   3.75
☐ Ice cream   2.75

Drinks
☐ Tea   1.50
☐ Soda   1.75
☐ Coffee   1.50
☐ Juice   2.00

2.

MENU

Appetizers
☐ Soup of the day   4.50
☐ Greek salad   5.00

Main Dishes
☐ Vegetable plate   9.50
☐ Grilled fish with
   broccoli or peas   13.00

Desserts
☐ Chocolate cake   3.75
☐ Ice cream   2.75

Drinks
☐ Iced tea   1.50
☐ Soda   1.75
☐ Coffee   1.50
☐ Juice   2.00

3.

MENU

Appetizers
☐ Chicken soup   2.75
☐ Spinach salad   3.50

Main Dishes
☐ Beef stir-fry   5.95
☐ Hamburger
   with fries   4.95

Desserts
☐ Cheesecake   3.50
☐ Fresh fruit   2.75

Drinks
☐ Coffee/Tea   1.50
☐ Milk   2.00
☐ Soda   1.75
☐ Juice   2.50

3. Let's Listen

People are having dinner. What does the waitress bring them?
Listen and check (✓) the correct picture.

1.

    a.   b.

2.

    a.   b.

3.

    a.   b.

4.

    a.   b.

5.

    a.   b.

6.

    a.   b.

Listen again. Was each customer pleased or not pleased with the order?
Check (✓) the correct answer.

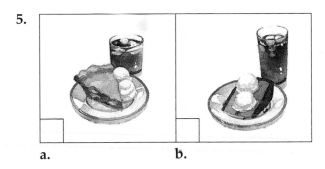

	Pleased	Not pleased
1. pizza	☐	☐
2. steak	☐	☐
3. chicken	☐	☐
4. vegetable	☐	☐
5. chocolate cake	☐	☐
6. spaghetti	☐	☐

4. Let's Listen

People are talking about meals they had at a restaurant. Did they like their meals? Listen and check (✓) the correct answer.

		Liked	Didn't like
1.	the appetizer	✓	☐
	the main dish	☐	☐
	the vegetables	☐	☐
	the dessert	☐	☐
2.	the appetizer	☐	☐
	the main dish	☐	☐
	the vegetables	☐	☐
	the dessert	☐	☐
3.	the appetizer	☐	☐
	the main dish	☐	☐
	the vegetables	☐	☐
	the dessert	☐	☐
4.	the appetizer	☐	☐
	the main dish	☐	☐
	the vegetables	☐	☐
	the dessert	☐	☐

Task 2

Listen again. Are these statements true or false? Check (✓) the correct answer.

		True	False
1.	The steak was a little tough.	☐	☐
2.	The cake was delicious.	☐	☐
3.	The steamed vegetables were perfect.	☐	☐
4.	The onion soup was too salty.	☐	☐

Over to You: Are you ready to order?

Task 1

Imagine that you are at your favorite restaurant. What will you order?
Write the answers in the menu.

MENU

Appetizer: _____

Main dish: _____

Dessert: _____

Drink: _____

Other: _____

Task 2

Work in pairs. Take turns being a waiter or waitress and a customer.
Use the suggestions below or use your own words. The waiter or
waitress writes the customer's answers on the order pad.

Waiter or Waitress:

　　Are you ready to order?

　　Would you like an appetizer?

　　What would you like for your main dish?

　　Would you like something to drink?

　　Any dessert?

　　Anything else?

Order

_____

Appetizer: _____

Main dish: _____

Dessert: _____

Drink: _____

Other: _____

Thank You!

Customer:

　　I'd like _____.

　　I'll have _____.

UNIT 13 Small Talk

1. Getting Ready

Read these expressions. How do people use them in conversation?
Check (✓) the correct answer.

		Greeting someone	Ending a conversation
1.	Keep in touch.	☐	✓
2.	How have you been?	☐	☐
3.	Well, it's been nice talking to you.	☐	☐
4.	How's everything?	☐	☐
5.	Hope to see you again soon.	☐	☐
6.	Well, talk to you later.	☐	☐
7.	Hello. Nice to see you again.	☐	☐
8.	Hey, how's it going?	☐	☐
9.	I haven't seen you for a long time.	☐	☐
10.	It's been great seeing you again.	☐	☐

2. Let's Listen

Listen to the conversations. Is each person greeting someone or ending a conversation?
Check (✓) the correct answer.

	Greeting someone	Ending a conversation
1.	☐	☐
2.	☐	☐
3.	☐	☐
4.	☐	☐
5.	☐	☐
6.	☐	☐
7.	☐	☐
8.	☐	☐

3. Let's Listen

Task 1

Some guests are talking at a party. What are they talking about? Listen and circle the correct answer.

1. **a.** the guests
   b. the music
   c. friends

2. **a.** a guest
   b. the music
   c. Jim

3. **a.** the music
   b. a guest
   c. an old friend

4. **a.** school
   b. the man's health
   c. work

5. **a.** a guest
   b. the party
   c. the food

6. **a.** a job
   b. a vacation
   c. friends

7. **a.** the guests
   b. her new job
   c. family

8. **a.** family
   b. the food
   c. the guests

Task 2

Listen again. Which statement is true? Circle the correct answer.

1. **a.** The woman is having a good time.
   b. The woman is not enjoying herself.
   c. The guests are unfriendly.

2. **a.** Jim does not recognize the singer.
   b. Jim does not like the singer.
   c. Jim likes the singer.

3. **a.** The man knows the guest.
   b. The man has not met the guest yet.
   c. The man does not want to meet the guest.

4. **a.** The man does not work now.
   b. The man is not busy now.
   c. The man is very busy now.

5. **a.** The man is hungry.
   b. The man does not want anything to eat.
   c. The man wants to drink.

6. **a.** The man took a train across the U.S.
   b. The man never travels.
   c. The man recently took a trip.

7. **a.** The woman's mother is not working now.
   b. The woman has a job now.
   c. The woman's mother has a new job.

8. **a.** The man knows a lot of people at the party.
   b. The man does not know a lot of people at the party.
   c. The man knows everyone at the party.

4. Let's Listen

Task 1

Two people are talking. Does the second speaker know the information or is it new information? Listen and check (✓) the correct answer.

	Known information	New information
1.	☐	☑
2.	☐	☐
3.	☐	☐
4.	☐	☐
5.	☐	☐
6.	☐	☐

Task 2

Listen again. Circle the correct answer.

1. a. Cindy has a new job.
   b. Cindy is going to change jobs.
   c. Cindy has just received a big raise.

2. a. The rock concert is next month.
   b. All the tickets have been sold.
   c. They don't like rock music.

3. a. The puppy was a birthday present.
   b. She had a dog before.
   c. She hasn't decided what to call the puppy yet.

4. a. Terry will be arriving later.
   b. Terry hasn't been sick this year.
   c. Terry has the flu.

5. a. He has acted in some movies.
   b. The guy lives in Canada.
   c. Both of them have already seen his movies.

6. a. The exhibition starts next month.
   b. The exhibition is about Walt Disney.
   c. They are not interested in cartoons.

Over to You: How's your family?

Work in pairs. Match the sentences on the left with the correct responses on the right. Write the letter. Then practice each conversation.

Example: A: How's your family these days?

B: They're fine, thanks. How is yours?

A

1. How's your family these days? ___

2. I haven't seen you for a long time. What have you been doing? ___

3. Great to see you. I hope to see you again soon. ___

4. Hey, it's been nice talking to you. Let's keep in touch. ___

B

a. Oh, not much really. I've been studying a lot.

b. They're fine, thanks. How is yours?

c. Yeah, let's talk again soon. I'll call you.

d. I hope so, too. How about lunch next week?

Task 2

Work in pairs. Pretend you have not seen your partner for a long time. You meet each other for lunch. Have a conversation with each other using the guidelines below.

1. Greet each other.

2. Ask and answer questions about the weather, your families, and what you have been doing.

3. End the conversation.

1. Getting Ready

When do you use these words and phrases? Write them in the correct lists.
Then add your own expressions to each list.

not bad	wonderful	very disappointing	nothing special	awful	all right
so-so	terrific	fantastic	pretty boring	really great	terrible

Didn't like it	Liked it a little	Liked it a lot
_____	*not bad*	_____
_____	_____	_____
_____	_____	_____
_____	_____	_____
_____	_____	_____

2. Let's Listen

These people didn't have a good vacation. What did they do? Listen and circle
the correct answer.

1. **a.** went away
   b. stayed home

2. **a.** went to Hawaii
   b. went to Okinawa

3. **a.** went away
   b. stayed home

4. **a.** invited relatives to stay
   b. visited relatives

5. **a.** went to the beach
   b. went to the country

6. **a.** went skiing
   b. stayed home

7. **a.** went skiing
   b. stayed home

8. **a.** went to Las Vegas
   b. went to Los Angeles

3. Let's Listen

Task 1

People are talking about their vacations. Did they enjoy them? Listen and check (✓)
the correct answer.

1. ☐ yes   3. ☐ yes   5. ☐ yes   7. ☐ yes
   ☐ no   ☐ no   ☐ no   ☐ no

2. ☐ yes   4. ☐ yes   6. ☐ yes   8. ☐ yes
   ☐ no   ☐ no   ☐ no   ☐ no

Task 2

Listen again. What word completes each statement? Write the correct letter.

1. The weather was _____ .   a. fantastic

2. The people were _____ .   b. terrible

3. The ski trip was _____ .   c. disappointing

4. Their trip to France was very _____ . d. nice

5. Her trip to the beach was _____ .   e. clean

6. The hotel wasn't _____ .   f. awful

7. The shopping in Thailand was _____ . g. short

8. His vacation was too _____ .   h. terrific

4. Let's Listen

Task 1

People are talking about their vacations. Listen and number the pictures.

A.

B.

C.

D. /

E.

F.

Task 2

Listen again. Are these statements true or false? Check (✓) the correct answer.

	True	False
1. She learned to water-ski very slowly.	☐	☐
2. It was cold at night.	☐	☐
3. The museums were interesting.	☐	☐
4. The weather wasn't good.	☐	☐
5. He went to France.	☐	☐
6. They had a comfortable trip.	☐	☐

Over to You: Your last vacation

Read the questions below and write the answers.

You	
1. Where did you go on your last vacation?	_____
2. When did you go there?	_____
3. Who did you go with?	_____
4. How long were you there?	_____
5. What did you do there?	_____
6. What did you enjoy the most?	_____
7. What didn't you like?	_____
8. What kinds of food did you try?	_____

Task 2

Work in pairs. Add two more questions to ask your partner about his or her last vacation. Then interview your partner. Write the answers in the chart.

Your partner	
1. Where did you go on your last vacation?	_____
2. When did you go there?	_____
3. Who did you go with?	_____
4. How long were you there?	_____
5. What did you do there?	_____
6. What did you enjoy the most?	_____
7. What didn't you like?	_____
8. What kinds of food did you try?	_____
9. _____	_____
10. _____	_____

1. Getting Ready

Where do you usually find these things in your apartment or house? Put the items in the lists. Then add one more item to each list.

toilet	bed	dresser	shower	refrigerator	piano
stove	sofa	coffee table	mattress	bathtub	microwave

Living room	Bedroom	Bathroom	Kitchen
_____	_____	*toilet*	_____
_____	_____	_____	_____
_____	_____	_____	_____
_____	_____	_____	_____

2. Let's Listen

People are describing their apartments. Listen and number the pictures.

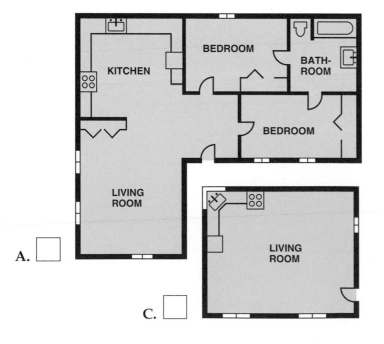

A. ☐

C. ☐

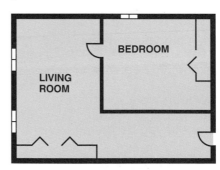

B. ☐

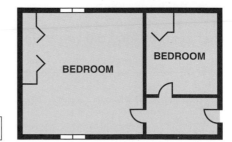

D. ☐

3. Let's Listen

Task 1

These people are describing rooms in their apartments. Listen and check (✓) the correct picture.

1.
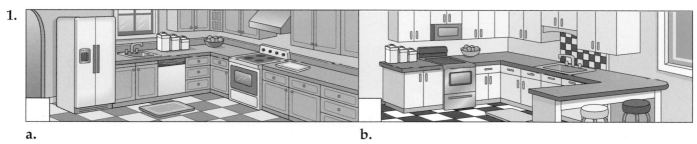

   a.   b.

2.

   a.   b.

3.

   a.   b.

4.
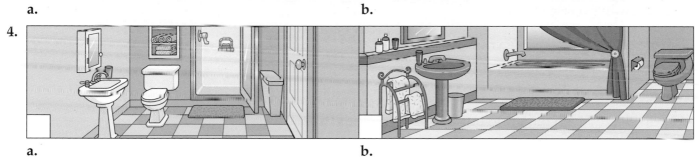

   a.   b.

Task 2

Listen again. Are these statements true or false? Check (✓) the correct answer.

	True	False
1. She doesn't plan to buy anything else for the apartment.	☐	☐
2. He has a new bed.	☐	☐
3. She wants to buy some more furniture.	☐	☐
4. She'll probably take a bath at her friend's place.	☐	☐

4. Let's Listen

Listen to people talking about their new apartments. What do they already have?
Check (✓) the correct answers.

		Bookshelf	TV	Stereo	Dinner table	Sofa
1.	Becky	✓	✓	☐	✓	☐
2.	Paul	☐	☐	☐	☐	☐
3.	Sarah	☐	☐	☐	☐	☐
4.	Sam	☐	☐	☐	☐	☐

Task 2

Listen again. Are these statements true or false? Check (✓) the correct answer.

		True	False
1. a.	She wants to buy a cheap stereo.	☐	☐
b.	She wants a large sofa.	☐	☐
2. a.	He wants to find a bigger bookshelf.	☐	☐
b.	He wants to find a cheaper dinner table.	☐	☐
3. a.	She doesn't have very many books yet.	☐	☐
b.	She has enough money to buy a stereo.	☐	☐
4. a.	He's waiting for the new TV models.	☐	☐
b.	He bought a dinner table last week.	☐	☐

Over to You: What's your favorite room?

Think about your favorite room and answer the questions.

1. What is your favorite room? _____

2. Why is it your favorite room? _____

3. What does it have in it? _____

4. How much time do you spend there? _____

5. What do you like to do there? _____

Task 2

Work in pairs. Describe a room in your home while your partner draws it.
Make sure your partner includes the details you describe.

Example: **A:** There is a sofa in the corner.

  B: Here?

  A: No. The other corner.

  B: Over here?

  A: Yes, that's right. And there's a big window
    above the sofa.

UNIT 16 Movies

1. Getting Ready

What kinds of movies do you like? Check (✓) your answers and compare them with a partner. Add one more kind of movie to the list.

	Like a lot	Like a little	Don't like
animated movie	☐	☐	☐
comedy	☐	☐	☐
horror	☐	☐	☐
western	☐	☐	☐
action	☐	☐	☐
romance	☐	☐	☐
musical	☐	☐	☐
other: _____	☐	☐	☐

2. Let's Listen

These people are talking about movies. What kinds of movies do they like?
Listen and check (✓) the correct answers.

	Science fiction	Horror	Comedy	Western	Action
1. Sue	☐	☐	☐	☐	☐
2. Bob	☐	☐	☐	☐	☐
3. Andrew	☐	☐	☐	☐	☐
4. Tina	☐	☐	☐	☐	☐

3. Let's Listen

Task 1

Listen to people talking about movies. Check (✓) the kind of movie they describe.

	Science fiction	Horror	Comedy	Romance	Action
1.	☐	☐	☐	☐	☐
2.	☐	☐	☐	☐	☐
3.	☐	☐	☐	☐	☐
4.	☐	☐	☐	☐	☐
5.	☐	☐	☐	☐	☐

Task 2

Listen again. Do you think the second speaker will see the movie or not? Check (✓) the correct answer.

	Will see it	Won't see it
1.	☐	☐
2.	☐	☐
3.	☐	☐
4.	☐	☐
5.	☐	☐

4. Let's Listen

Task 1

Listen to people talking about movies they have seen. Check (✓) what they liked about each movie.

	The actors	The story	The music	The special effects
1.	☐	☐	☐	☐
2.	☐	☐	☐	☐
3.	☐	☐	☐	☐
4.	☐	☐	☐	☐

Task 2

Listen again. Where does each story take place? Write the correct letter.

1. ___   **a.** Kansas

2. ___   **b.** Africa

3. ___   **c.** San Francisco

4. ___   **d.** London

Over to You: Movie survey

Answer the questions. Then add two questions of your own.

1. How often do you go to movies?
   (once a week, twice a month, three times a year) _____

2. What kind of movies do you like? _____

3. What kind don't you like? _____

4. Write the name of a movie you really loved. _____

5. Who were the stars in it? _____

6. Name an actor you really like. _____

7. Name an actress you really like. _____

8. Do you prefer going out to movies or
   watching videos at home? _____

9. What kind of movie would you like to star in? _____

10. Who would you choose to star with you? Why? _____

11. _____ _____

12. _____ _____

Task 2

Work in groups of four. Ask each other the questions in the chart.

UNIT 17 The Weather

1. Getting Ready

What's the weather like in your town or city? Read the words and write them in the correct column. Then add your own words.

rainy	dry	warm	cloudy	cold	humid
hot	sunny	cool	windy	wet	snowy

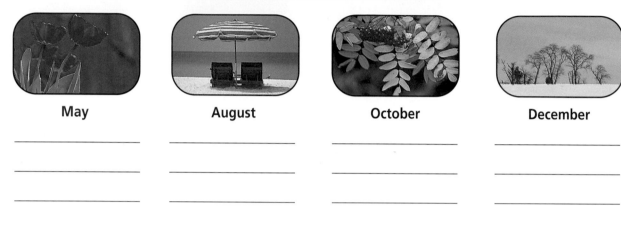

May   August   October   December

_____   _____   _____   _____

_____   _____   _____   _____

_____   _____   _____   _____

_____   _____   _____   _____

2. Let's Listen

Task 1

Listen to these weather reports and check (✓) the weather for each city.

City	Weather			
1. Beijing	✓ cold	✓ windy	☐ snowy	☐ cool
2. Mexico City	☐ dry	☐ warm	☐ cool	☐ wet
3. Tokyo	☐ humid	☐ cloudy	☐ windy	☐ rainy
4. New York	☐ sunny	☐ windy	☐ wet	☐ cold
5. Taipei	☐ cloudy	☐ cool	☐ wet	☐ hot

Task 2

Listen again. Write the temperatures.

City	Low	High
1. Beijing	0°	6°
2. Mexico City	_____	_____
3. Tokyo	_____	_____
4. New York	_____	_____
5. Taipei	_____	_____

3. Let's Listen

These people are asking about the weather. What will they wear or take with them?
Listen and check (✓) the correct picture.

1.

a.   b.

2.

a.   b.

3.
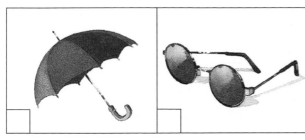
a.   b.

4.
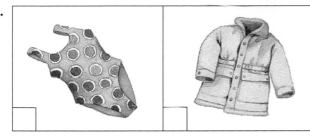
a.   b.

5.

a.   b.

6.
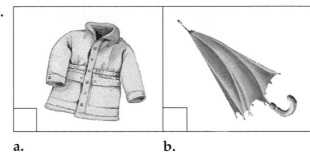
a.   b.

Listen again. Circle the answer that does <u>not</u> describe the weather now.

1. **a.** It's raining.
   b. It's windy.
   c. It's cloudy.

2. **a.** It's cloudy.
   b. It's nice.
   c. It's sunny.

3. **a.** It's cold.
   b. It's warm.
   c. It's snowing.

4. **a.** It's icy.
   b. It's nice.
   c. It's raining.

5. **a.** It's humid.
   b. It's raining.
   c. It's hot.

6. **a.** It's snowing.
   b. It's windy.
   c. It's cold.

4. Let's Listen

Task 1

These people are talking about the weather. What is it like now?
Listen and circle the correct answer.

1. **a.** It's warm.
   b. It's windy.

2. **a.** It's windy.
   b. It's getting warmer.

3. **a.** The sky is dark.
   b. It's sunny.

4. **a.** It's windy.
   b. It's sunny.

5. **a.** It's cold.
   b. It's really nice.

6. **a.** It's raining.
   b. It's not raining.

7. **a.** It's getting cooler.
   b. It's hot.

8. **a.** It's raining.
   b. It's snowing.

Task 2

Listen again. Is the weather getting better or worse? Check (✓) the correct answer.

	Better	Worse		Better	Worse
1.	☐	☐	**5.**	☐	☐
2.	☐	☐	**6.**	☐	☐
3.	☐	☐	**7.**	☐	☐
4.	☐	☐	**8.**	☐	☐

Over to You: Fun things to do

Task 1

Work in pairs. Think of two fun things to do on each of the days below.
Write them in the chart.

Example: A fun thing to do on a cool, sunny spring day is go hiking.

Type of day	Activities	
1. a cool, sunny day	_____	_____
2. a cool, rainy day	_____	_____
3. a hot, rainy day	_____	_____
4. a hot, sunny day	_____	_____
5. a cold, snowy day	_____	_____
6. a cold, sunny day	_____	_____

Task 2

Work in groups of four. Now compare your activities with two other pairs. Which
activities did they have that you did not? Write those activities in the chart.

Type of day	Activities	
1. a cool, sunny day	_____	_____
2. a cool, rainy day	_____	_____
3. a hot, rainy day	_____	_____
4. a hot, sunny day	_____	_____
5. a cold, snowy day	_____	_____
6. a cold, sunny day	_____	_____

UNIT 18 Shopping

1. Getting Ready

Where can you buy the items below? Match the item on the left with a store on the right. Write one more item you can buy in each store.

1. CD _c_

2. magazines ___

3. tie ___

4. necklace ___

5. vegetables ___

6. envelopes ___

7. running shoes ___

a. jewelry store _____

b. bookstore _____

c. music store _____

d. clothing store _____

e. grocery store _____

f. sporting goods store _____

g. stationery store _____

2. Let's Listen

People are talking as they shop. Listen and number the pictures.

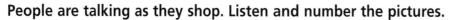

A.

B.

C.

D.

E.

F.

3. Let's Listen

Task 1

Customers are talking to salespeople in a store. Do the customers make a purchase? Listen and check (✓) the correct answer.

1. ☐ yes   3. ☐ yes   5. ☐ yes   7. ☐ yes
    ☐ no   ☐ no   ☐ no   ☐ no

2. ☐ yes   4. ☐ yes   6. ☐ yes   8. ☐ yes
    ☐ no   ☐ no   ☐ no   ☐ no

Task 2

Listen again. What do you think the clerk says next? Circle the correct answer.

1. a. Okay. It's $37.50 with tax.
   b. Let me know if you need help.

2. a. You're welcome.
   b. Cash or credit?

3. a. You're welcome.
   b. Can I show you something else?

4. a. Why not?
   b. Okay. Let me know if I can help you.

5. a. Let me put it in a box for you.
   b. Let me check.

6. a. Great! Let me know if I can help you.
   b. Great! I'll ring it up for you.

7. a. Let me know if you need help.
   b. How many do you need?

8. a. Would you like to pay with cash?
   b. We may get more next week.

4. Let's Listen

Task 1

These people are asking about items in a store. Listen and check (✓) the item they talk about.

1.
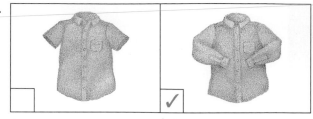

a.   b. ✓

2.
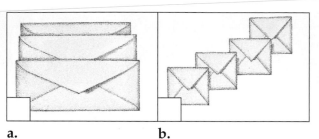

a.   b.

3.
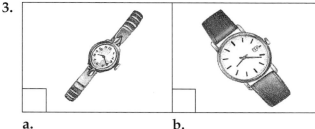

a.   b.

4.
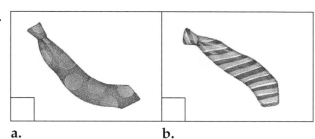

a.   b.

5.
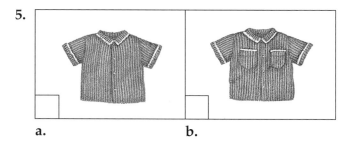

a.   b.

6.

a.   b.

Task 2

Listen again. Circle the correct answer.

1. **a.** You can machine-wash the shirt.
   b. It's best to dry-clean it.
   c. You can hand-wash it.

2. **a.** They are regular mail envelopes.
   b. They can also be used for air mail.
   c. They can be used for air mail and regular mail.

3. **a.** The man wants the watch for himself.
   b. It's not a woman's watch.
   c. Either a man or a woman can wear the watch.

4. **a.** The man likes both ties.
   b. The woman prefers the striped tie.
   c. The tie is a gift for someone.

5. **a.** The blouse is made of cotton.
   b. The blouse is made of cotton and linen.
   c. The blouse is made of linen.

6. **a.** The large apples aren't very sweet.
   b. Both types of apples are usually sweet.
   c. They don't like sweet apples.

Over to You: Where's a good place to buy...?

Work in groups of four. Where is a good place in your town or city to buy the items listed? Write suggestions for each item. Then compare your suggestions with those of another group.

Example: **A:** Where's a good place to buy _____?

B: Well, you can buy them at _____ .

C: You can also get them at _____ .

D: I think the best place is _____ .

A: I think so, too.

Item	Your group's suggestions	Other group's suggestions
jeans		
books		
shoes		
birthday cards		
computer software		
cameras		
sports equipment		
jewelry		
CDs		
makeup		

UNIT 19 Using the Telephone

1. Getting Ready

Match the questions on the left with the answers on the right.

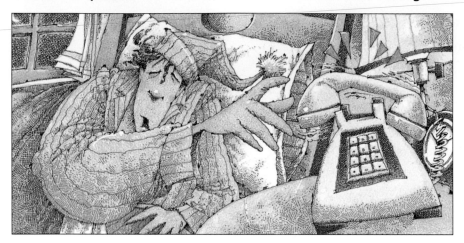

1. May I ask who is calling? _e_
2. What number did you want? ___
3. Do you want to leave a message? ___
4. Is this 891-2168? ___
5. Can I speak to Michael, please? ___

a. 319-8216.
b. Yes, just a minute, please.
c. No, it isn't. I think you have the wrong number.
d. No, I'll call back. Thanks.
e. This is Tom Foster.

2. Let's Listen

Which statement about each telephone call is true? Listen and circle the correct answer.

1. a. Joe is busy.
   b. It's a wrong number.

2. a. Sandy is not free.
   b. Sandy is not in.

3. a. It's a wrong number.
   b. Brian is not home.

4. a. It's a wrong number.
   b. Sylvia is out.

5. a. Mrs. Brown can't come to the phone.
   b. Mrs. Brown is home.

6. a. Tony can't come to the phone.
   b. Tony is in.

3. Let's Listen

Read these telephone messages. Then listen and correct the mistakes in each message.

1.

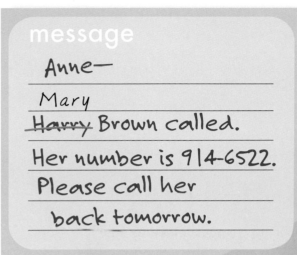

message

Anne—

Mary

~~Harry~~ Brown called.

Her number is 914-6522.

Please call her

back tomorrow.

2.

message

John—

Helen called.

Her number is 614-5553.

Meet her at 12 o'clock

tomorrow at the library.

3.

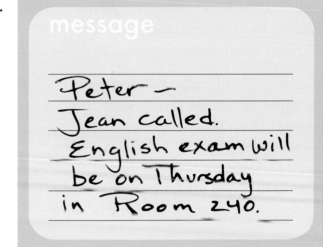

message

Peter —

Jean called.

English exam will

be on Thursday

in Room 240.

4.

message

Patrick—

Jon called.

Tonight's party

is at 7:00 at

the Plaza Hotel.

Listen again. Circle the correct information.

1. a. Anne is in, but she can't come to the phone.
   b. Anne isn't in now.
   c. Anne won't be back tonight.

2. a. John is still at school.
   b. John is out buying books.
   c. John doesn't know Ellen.

3. a. Peter is making dinner.
   b. Peter is out for the evening.
   c. Peter will be back soon.

4. a. Patrick is sleeping.
   b. Patrick will call back tonight.
   c. Patrick is eating dinner.

4. Let's Listen

Task 1

Listen to each conversation. What is each call about? Circle the correct answer.

1. **a.** an apology for missing a movie
   b. an invitation to a movie
   c. a cancellation of a movie

2. **a.** a suggestion about a stereo
   b. a request to borrow a stereo
   c. a complaint about a stereo

3. **a.** a complaint about a date
   b. an invitation to go on a date
   c. a cancellation of a date

4. **a.** a request to change a meeting time
   b. an offer to change a meeting time
   c. a promise to change a meeting time

5. **a.** a suggestion about where to have dinner
   b. an apology for missing dinner
   c. a complaint about dinner

6. **a.** a complaint about helping Becky move
   b. an invitation to help Becky move
   c. a promise to help Becky move

Task 2

Listen again. Is each person pleased or not pleased after getting the call?
Check (✓) the correct answer.

1. ☐ pleased
   ☐ not pleased

2. ☐ pleased
   ☐ not pleased

3. ☐ pleased
   ☐ not pleased

4. ☐ pleased
   ☐ not pleased

5. ☐ pleased
   ☐ not pleased

6. ☐ pleased
   ☐ not pleased

Over to You: Can I leave a message, please?

Task 1

Work in pairs. Number the sentences in A and B to make a telephone conversation.
Then practice the conversation with your partner.

A

___ Okay. I'll give her the message.

___ I'm sorry. She's not at home right now.

___ Sure. Just let me get a pen and some paper.

_1_ Hello.

___ You're welcome. Good-bye.

___ Does she have your telephone number?

B

___ Yes, she does.

___ Good-bye.

___ Can you tell her that Bob called? And please ask her to call me back.

_2_ Hello. Can I speak to Cindy, please?

___ Oh, can I leave a message, please?

___ Thanks very much.

Task 2

Work in pairs. Think of three people you called last week and complete the charts.
Then take turns asking and answering the questions in the charts.

Call 1

Who did you call? _____

When did you call? _____

Why did you call? _____

Call 2

Who did you call? _____

When did you call? _____

Why did you call? _____

Call 3

Who did you call? _____

When did you call? _____

Why did you call? _____

Unit 19

77

UNIT 20 Describing Things

1. Getting Ready

Find these items in the picture. Write the letter next to each item.

1. a briefcase with initials *A*
2. a handbag with a leather strap ___
3. a small suitcase with a checked design ___
4. a large suitcase with wheels ___
5. a backpack with a striped design ___
6. a wallet without initials ___

2. Let's Listen

These people are describing items they left in a taxi. Listen and check (✓) the correct picture.

1.
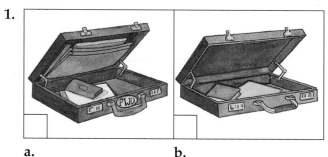

  a.   b.

2.
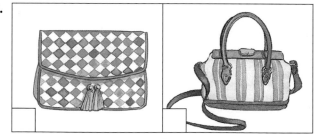

  a.   b.

3.
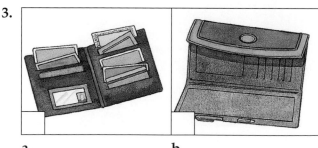

  a.   b.

4.
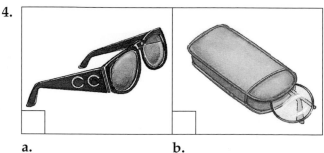

  a.   b.

3. Let's Listen

People are describing these items. Listen and number the pictures.

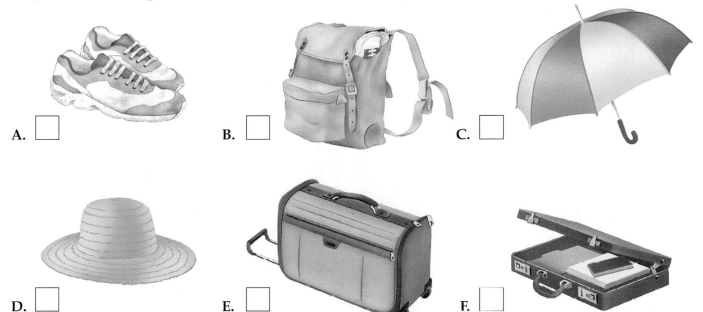

A. ☐   B. ☐   C. ☐

D. ☐   E. ☐   F. ☐

Task 2

Listen again. Why does each person like the item? Circle the correct information.

1. a. She wears it every day.
   b. The sun hurts her eyes.
   c. It's good for windy days.

2. a. It's made of plastic.
   b. It's small.
   c. It's great for work.

3. a. It's small.
   b. It's big.
   c. She uses it while she runs.

4. a. It's cheap.
   b. It's not easily seen.
   c. She likes the colors.

5. a. It doesn't have wheels.
   b. It's good for traveling.
   c. It's very big.

6. a. They're comfortable.
   b. They're new.
   c. He likes the color.

4. Let's Listen

Task 1

People are talking about items they lost. Listen and check (✓) the item each person describes.

Lost items
1. ✓ wallet
☐ suitcase
☐ beach bag
2. ☐ shoes
☐ keys
☐ glasses
3. ☐ keys
☐ rings
☐ pocket knife
4. ☐ suitcase
☐ credit card
☐ passport
5. ☐ passport
☐ suitcase
☐ jacket
6. ☐ novel
☐ newspaper
☐ letter

Task 2

Listen again. Where was each item lost? Circle the correct answer.

1. **a.** the bus
   b. the car

2. **a.** the bus
   b. the coffee shop

3. **a.** the school
   b. the house

4. **a.** the department store
   b. the restaurant

5. **a.** at home
   b. at the office

6. **a.** the subway
   b. at home

Over to You: What does it look like?

**Work in pairs. Take turns describing one of the items in each set of pictures.
Can your partner guess which item you are describing?**

Example: **A:** It's a leather briefcase with the initials MGL on it.

B: Is it *A*?

A: No, it doesn't have a long strap.

B: Oh, then is it *B*?

A: Yes, it is.

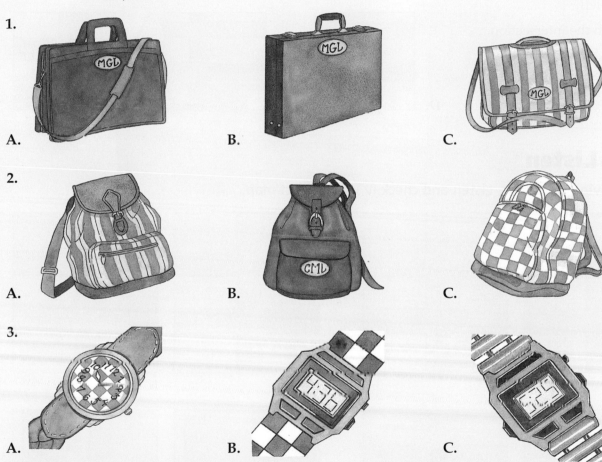

1.

A. B. C.

2.

A. B. C.

3.

A. B. C.

Task 2

**Work in pairs. Think of three items in your classroom. Give short clues and have
your partner try to guess the items.**

Example: **A:** It's rectangular.

B: Is it the teacher's desk?

A: No, it isn't. It's smaller.

B: Is it your desk?

A: Yes, it is.

UNIT 21 Directions

1. Getting Ready

Match each direction with a map. Write the number next to each map.

1. Go straight up the block.

2. Turn right at the light.

3. Take the first street on the left.

4. Go straight for two blocks. Then turn left.

5. Go through the intersection.

6. Take a right at the corner.

A. ☐ /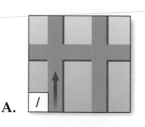

B. ☐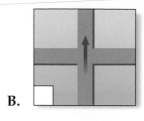

C. ☐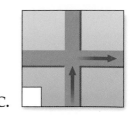

D. ☐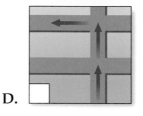

E. ☐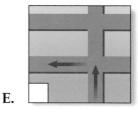

F. ☐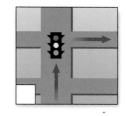

2. Let's Listen 💿

People are giving directions. Listen and check (✓) the correct map.

1.

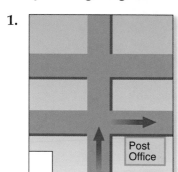
a.

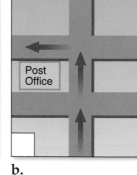
b.

2.

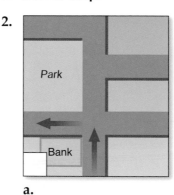
a.   b.

3.

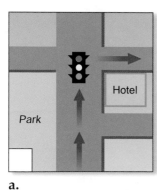
a.   b.

4.

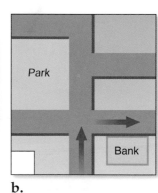
a.

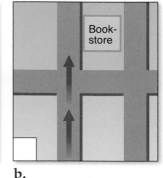
b.

3. Let's Listen

Task 1

Look at the map and listen to the directions. Write the number of each place on the map as you listen.

1. a bank
2. the Peking Restaurant
3. a supermarket

4. the post office
5. the tourist office
6. the art museum

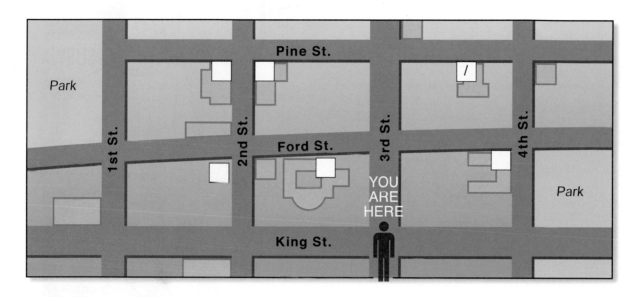

Task 2

Listen again. Complete the statements for each set of directions.

1. Go _straight_ up Third Street for two _blocks_ and _turn_ right on Pine Street.

2. It's _____ your left, on the _____ of Ford and Second.

3. Go left _____ King and _____ go _____ Second Street for two blocks.

4. It's not far _____ here.

5. Go up Third Street and turn _____ on Ford. It's in the first big building you see

   on your _____ .

6. Go to the _____ of the block.

4. Let's Listen

People are giving directions to their homes. Number the directions in the correct order.

1. Go down the street and my house is on the left. ___

   Walk past the hotel for two blocks. ___

   Come out of the subway. _1_

   You'll see a small street on the right. ___

2. Cross the footbridge. ___

   Go down the street on the other side of the footbridge. ___

   Get off the bus across from the supermarket. ___

   Walk north for two blocks. ___

3. Go down the street until you see the supermarket. ___

   Walk towards the river. ___

   Take the first street on the left. ___

   Go through the intersection. ___

4. Get off the bus across from the school. ___

   Go down the street until you see a church. ___

   Turn right just past the gas station. ___

   Walk north for about four blocks. ___

Task 2

Listen again. What should each person bring?
Circle the correct answer.

1. **a.** food
   b. CDs
   c. videos

2. **a.** snacks
   b. soda
   c. music

3. **a.** vegetables
   b. chips
   c. fruit

4. **a.** sneakers
   b. balls
   c. racket

Over to You: I'm looking for...

Ask your partner directions to the places on your list. Write the correct letter or number on your map.

Example: **Student A:** Excuse me. I'm looking for the Grand Hotel.

                       Student B: The Grand Hotel? Okay. Go straight up 1st street...

                       Student B: Excuse me. I'm trying to find a bank.

                       Student A: A bank? Let's see. Go up 1st Street...

Student A:

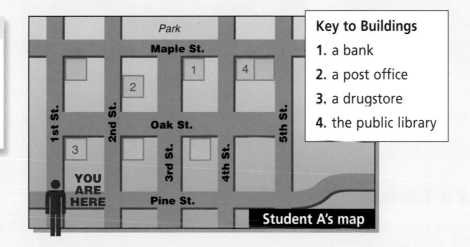

Student A's List

a. the Grand Hotel
b. the bookstore
c. the subway
d. the coffee shop

Key to Buildings

1. a bank
2. a post office
3. a drugstore
4. the public library

Student B:

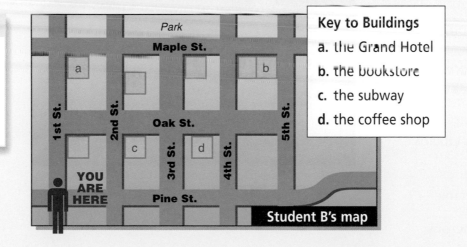

Student B's List

1. a bank
2. a post office
3. a drugstore
4. the public library

Key to Buildings

a. the Grand Hotel
b. the bookstore
c. the subway
d. the coffee shop

UNIT 22 People We Know

1. Getting Ready

What's your best friend like? Check (✓) words on the list that describe him or her.
Compare answers with a partner.

- ☐ shy
- ☐ talkative
- ☐ serious
- ☐ funny
- ☐ smart
- ☐ sociable
- ☐ easygoing
- ☐ a little crazy at times
- ☐ hardworking
- ☐ generous
- ☐ lazy
- ☐ kind

2. Let's Listen

These people are talking about new friends. Listen and circle the best word or phrase
to describe each person.

1. **a.** serious
   b. funny

2. **a.** shy
   b. talkative

3. **a.** serious
   b. crazy

4. **a.** smart
   b. not talkative

5. **a.** serious
   b. sociable

6. **a.** generous
   b. hardworking

3. Let's Listen

Are the people in each conversation similar or different? Listen and check (✓) the correct answer.

1. ☐ similar   3. ☐ similar   5. ☐ similar
   ☐ different   ☐ different   ☐ different

2. ☐ similar   4. ☐ similar   6. ☐ similar
   ☐ different   ☐ different   ☐ different

Task 2

Listen again. What do you think is true about each person? Circle the correct answer.

1. **a.** Mr. Grant is funny.
   b. Mrs. Grant loves to have fun.

2. **a.** Neither brother likes studying
   b. Both brothers go to school every day.

3. **a.** Mr. Roberts doesn't talk a lot.
   b. It's difficult to talk to Mrs. Roberts.

4. **a.** Wendy's boyfriend is very serious all the time.
   b. Wendy loves to have fun.

5. **a.** Both teachers are very easygoing.
   b. Both teachers just started teaching at the school.

6. **a.** The wife finishes work earlier than her husband.
   b. The husband works as hard as the wife.

4. Let's Listen

Mary is telling Anne about people at her school. What does she like or not like about each person? Listen and check (✓) the correct answer.

	Likes	Doesn't like
1. personality	✓	☐
sense of humor	☐	☐
habits	☐	☐

	Likes	Doesn't like
2. personality	☐	☐
sense of humor	☐	☐
habits	☐	☐

	Likes	Doesn't like
3. personality	☐	☐
sense of humor	☐	☐
habits	☐	☐

	Likes	Doesn't like
4. personality	☐	☐
sense of humor	☐	☐
habits	☐	☐

Listen again. Does Anne want to know each person? Check (✓) the correct answer.

1. ☐ yes   2. ☐ yes   3. ☐ yes   4. ☐ yes
   ☐ no   ☐ no   ☐ no   ☐ no

Over to You: What are you like?

What are you like? Check (✓) the answers in the chart.

You are...	Very	A little	Not at all
shy	☐	☐	☐
easygoing	☐	☐	☐
serious	☐	☐	☐
hardworking	☐	☐	☐
funny	☐	☐	☐
crazy at times	☐	☐	☐
lazy	☐	☐	☐
talkative	☐	☐	☐
kind	☐	☐	☐
other: _____	☐	☐	☐

Task 2

Work in pairs. What's your partner like? Guess by checking (✓) your answers in the chart.

Your partner is...	Very	A little	Not at all
shy	☐	☐	☐
easygoing	☐	☐	☐
serious	☐	☐	☐
hardworking	☐	☐	☐
funny	☐	☐	☐
crazy at times	☐	☐	☐
lazy	☐	☐	☐
talkative	☐	☐	☐
kind	☐	☐	☐
other: _____	☐	☐	☐

Now ask your partner about his or her qualities. Circle the qualities you guessed correctly and tell your partner what you guessed.

Example: A: Do you think you're shy?

B: Yes, I think I'm very shy.

A: I guessed you aren't shy at all./I guessed right.

How many did you guess correctly? ____

4. Let's Listen 💿

People are comparing two cities. Listen and circle the city each person prefers.

1. **a.** Washington, D.C.
   b. New York

2. **a.** Los Angeles
   b. San Francisco

3. **a.** Singapore
   b. Hong Kong

4. **a.** Sydney
   b. Melbourne

Task 2

Listen again. Which city do the words describe? Check (✓) the correct answer.

1.

	Washington, D.C.	New York
more exciting	☐	☐
more beautiful	☐	☐
cheaper restaurants	☐	☐
better theater	☐	☐

3.

	Singapore	Hong Kong
more beautiful	☐	☐
more comfortable	☐	☐
clean	☐	☐
polluted	☐	☐

2.

	Los Angeles	San Francisco
huge	☐	☐
more beautiful	☐	☐
boring	☐	☐
fast-moving	☐	☐

4.

	Sydney	Melbourne
more exciting	☐	☐
beautiful	☐	☐
better prices	☐	☐
more relaxing	☐	☐

Over to You: Create a travel brochure

**Work in pairs. Complete the travel brochure about a place you know.
Then compare your travel brochure with another pair.**

IT DOESN'T GET
any better than this!

Have you visited _____ lately?
Come and visit us soon. We promise you a great vacation.
We have great places for you to visit such as _____
_____
_____.

Our hotels are good, too. You can choose from _____
_____.

And there are a lot of interesting things to do and see here
such as _____
_____.

And you'll like our food. Don't forget to try _____
_____
_____.

Shopping is good, too. You can buy _____
_____
_____.

So come and visit us soon! We look forward _____
to seeing you in _____
_____.

UNIT 24 Health

1. Getting Ready

Match each word with the body part in the picture. Write the correct letter.

1. hand _J_
2. ear ___
3. mouth ___
4. nose ___
5. eye ___
6. foot ___
7. back ___
8. teeth ___
9. arm ___
10. head ___
11. leg ___
12. stomach ___
13. finger ___
14. toe ___

2. Let's Listen

People are talking about health problems. Listen and number the pictures.

A. ☐

B. ☐

C. ☐

D. ☐

E. ☐

F. ☐

3. Let's Listen

Task 1

Listen to people talking about health problems. What is each person's problem?
Write the correct letter.

1. Rick ___   a. a twisted ankle

2. Judy ___   b. a cut

3. Nancy ___   c. a stomachache

4. Tom ___   d. a backache

5. Renee ___   e. the flu

Task 2

Listen again. When did the problem start? Circle the correct answer.

1. a. last weekend   3. a. yesterday   5. a. last week
   b. yesterday   b. last week   b. last night
   c. two days ago   c. a few days ago   c. today

2. a. yesterday   4. a. today
   b. two days ago   b. last night
   c. today   c. a few days ago

4. Let's Listen

Task 1

Listen to people describing a health problem to a friend. What phrase completes each statement? Circle the correct answer.

1. Lately, she _____.

   a. easily falls asleep
   b. can't fall asleep
   c. sleeps all night

2. Lately, he doesn't _____.

   a. take any vitamins
   b. feel tired
   c. have any energy

3. She gets very bad _____.

   a. backaches
   b. headaches
   c. pains in her eyes

4. He's getting a lot of _____ this year.

   a. toothaches
   b. stomachaches
   c. colds

Task 2

Listen again. Circle what the friend suggests for each problem.

1. a. get something from the drug store
   b. get up and do something
   c. take sleeping pills

2. a. get more sleep
   b. see the doctor
   c. take vitamins

3. a. buy a new computer
   b. sit in a different way
   c. stop using the computer

4. a. take vitamin C
   b. go to the doctor
   c. get more exercise

Over to You: Guess what's wrong

Task 1

Work in pairs. Take turns. One person acts out a health problem. The other person guesses what it is. Use the health problems below or use your own ideas.

a headache	a cold	the flu	a backache	a stomachache
a toothache	an earache	a sore throat	a sore knee	

Task 2

Work in pairs. List five tips to stay healthy. Share them with another pair.

1. _____

2. _____

3. _____

4. _____

5. _____